★ It's My State! ★ ★ ★ ★ ★

MONTANA

The Treasure State

Ruth Bjorklund, Ellen H. Todras, and Gerry Boehme

Cavendish
Square

New York

Published in 2016 by Cavendish Square Publishing, LLC
243 5th Avenue, Suite 136, New York, NY 10016

Copyright © 2016 by Cavendish Square Publishing, LLC

First Edition

CPSIA Compliance Information: Batch #CW16CSQ

All websites were available and accurate when this book was sent to press.

Library of Congress Cataloging-in-Publication Data

Bjorklund, Ruth, author.
Montana / Ruth Bjorklund, Ellen H. Todras, and Gerry Boehme.
pages cm. — (It's my state!)
Includes index.
ISBN 978-1-6271-3204-6 (hardcover) — ISBN 978-1-6271-3206-0 (ebook)
1. Montana—History—Juvenile literature. I. Todras, Ellen H., 1947- author. II. Boehme, Gerry, author. III. Title.

F731.3.B54 2016
978.6—dc23

2015032373

Editorial Director: David McNamara
Editor: Fletcher Doyle
Copy Editor: Nathan Heidelberger
Art Director: Jeffrey Talbot
Designer: Stephanie Flecha
Senior Production Manager: Jennifer Ryder-Talbot
Production Editor: Renni Johnson
Photo Research: J8 Media

The photographs in this book are used by permission and through the courtesy of: Natalia Bratslavsky/Shutterstock.com, cover; Peter Wey/Shutterstock.com, 4; Matt Knoth/Shutterstock.com, 4; JMichl/iStockphoto.com, 4; brewbooks (http://www.flickr.com/people/93452909@N00) from near Seattle, USA/File:Flickr - brewbooks - Lewisia rediviva (Bitterroot) on Tronsen Ridge.jpg/Wikimedia Commons, 5; Ken Lucas/Getty Images, 5; Tom Grundy/Shutterstock.com, 5; Danita Delimont/Getty Images, 6; welcomia/Shutterstock.com, 8; Wayne Scherr/Getty Images, 9; Tom Danneman/Getty Images, 11; Travel Ink/Getty Images, 12; Pierdelune/Shutterstock.com, 13; Woods Wheatcroft/Aurora/Getty Images, 4; National Park Service Digital Image Archives/File:Grant-Kohrs Ranch National Historic Site GRKO3395.jpg/Wikimedia Commons, 14; Wayne Scherr/Getty Images, 14; AHPix/Shutterstock.com, 15; Richard Cummins/Lonely Planet/Getty Images, 15; Radoslaw Lecyk/Shutterstock.com, 15; David Marx/Shutterstock.com, 16; Anthony Spencer/Vetta/Getty Images, 18; Tom Reichner/Shutterstock.com, 20; Megan Malone/Taxi/Getty Images, 20; James Steinberg/Getty Images, 20, Thinkstock, 21; Tom McHugh/Shutterstock.com, 21; Matt Jeppson/Shutterstock.com, 21; David Parsons/iStockphoto.com, 22; Werner Forman/Art Resource, 24; David Gallery/Getty Images, 25; Lawrence Migdale/Getty Images, 26; Robert Kyllo/Shutterstock.com, 28; North Wind Picture Archives, 29; Julie Alissi/J8 Media, 30; MPI/Archive Photos/Getty Images, 32; William A. Allard/National Geographic Image Collection/Getty Images, 33; Walter Bibikow/AWL Images/Getty Images, 34; Patti McConville/Getty Images, 345; Jeff the quiet/File:Kalispell Main Street.jpg/Wikimedia Coimmons, 35; Stephen Saks Photography/Alamy, 35; PhotoQuest/Getty Images, 37; Fotosearch/Superstock, 38; Margaret Bourke-White/Getty Images, 40; AP Photo/Billings Gazette, Layer Mayer/Alamy, 41; Gordon Wiltsie/National Geographic Image Collection/Getty Images, 44; Danita Delimont/Gallo Images, 46; Matthew Brady/File:Pierre-Jean De Smet - Brady-Handy.jpg/Wikimedia Commons, 47; Valerie Macon/Getty Images, 48; Michael Loccisano/Getty Images, 48; AP Photo/Great Falls Tribune, 48; Brad Barket/Getty Images, 49; John Lamparski/Getty Images, 49; Ian Gaven/Getty Images, 49; Accurate Art, 50; Visions of America/Superstock, 52; William Albert Allard/National Geographic/Getty Images, 54; emattil/Shutterstock.com, 54; AP Photo/Great Falls Tribune, 55; AP Photo/The Montana Standard, 55; Nagel Photography/Shutterstock.com, 56; Parkerdr/File:MontanaOriginalGovernorsMansion.jpg/Wikimedia Commons, 58; AP Photo/The Independent Record, 60; AP Photo/Matt Volz, 61; Harry E. Walker/MCT via Getty Images, 62 AP Photo/Sadayuki Mikami, 62; FPG/Archive Photos/Getty Images, 62; Jim Gipe/AGE Fotostock, 64; AP Photo, 66; Cavan Images/Iconica/Getty Images, 69; AP Photo/Nati Harnik, 69; Eastcott Momatiuk/Image Bank/Getty Images, 70; AP Photo/Susan Gallagher, 69; Teri Virbickis/Shutterstock.com, 70; Michael Melford/National Geographic Image Collection/Getty Images, 71; Danita Delimont†/Alamy, 72; Shannonfreix/File:Volunteer on the CDT.JPG/Wikimedia Commons, 73; Christopher Santoro, 74, 75 (seal and flag); jfisher2167 (http://www.flickr.com/people/62080220@N04)/ File:Granite Peak Montana 2.jpg/Wikimedia Commons, 75; USACE photographer/File:Fort Peck Lake.jpeg, 75.

Printed in the United States of America

MONTANA
CONTENTS

A QUICK LOOK AT

State Animal: Grizzly Bear

Grizzlies range in color from blond to dark brown and black. Grizzlies are omnivores, which means that they eat both plants and animals. Grizzlies can weigh from 200 to 800 pounds (90 to 360 kilograms), but despite their size, they can run up to 35 miles per hour (56 kilometers per hour).

State Bird: Western Meadowlark

The western meadowlark is a brightly colored black and yellow songbird that lives in meadows and perches on fence posts throughout the state. It eats seeds, grains, caterpillars, cutworms, grasshoppers, and other insects. This bird builds a nest of grass and bark on the ground, woven into the surrounding plants.

State Fish: Blackspotted Cutthroat Trout

The blackspotted cutthroat trout has black spots that run down its back and pinkish-red streaks under its jaw. Trout are opportunistic feeders, which means they will eat a lot of different things to stay alive. This fish is a favorite food for people and also for grizzly bears.

MONTANA
POPULATION: 989,415

⭐ State Flower: Bitterroot

Bitterroot is a small, low-growing, pink wildflower. Its scientific name is *Lewisia rediviva*, in honor of American explorer Meriwether Lewis, who collected the plant in Montana in 1806. The root of the plant was important in the diet of Native Americans, who considered it a valuable trade item.

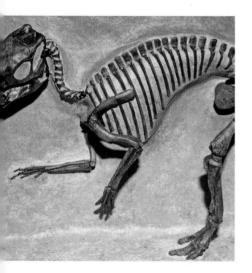

⭐ State Fossil: *Maiasaura*

The duck-billed dinosaur *Maiasaura* lived about one hundred million to sixty-five million years ago. The name *Maiasaura* means "good mother lizard" in Greek. *Maiasaura* fossils provided the first evidence that dinosaurs cared for their young, much as birds do now. Adult *Maiasaura* weighed about 6,000 pounds (2,700 kg).

⭐ State Tree: Ponderosa Pine

One of the most common trees in the western United States, the ponderosa pine got its name because it is so large and heavy, or ponderous. Reaching heights of 100 to 150 feet (30 to 45 meters), ponderosa pine timber was used by settlers to make everything from railroad ties to homes.

Daybreak colors the badlands of eastern Montana near Fort Peck Lake.

The Treasure State

Montanan A. B. Guthrie Jr., author of the 1947 Western novel *The Big Sky*, once remarked, "I've always thought of Montana as my center of the universe." With a land area of 145,546 square miles (376,962 square kilometers), Montana is the fourth-largest state in the nation. Montana is as large as or larger than such countries as Germany, Ecuador, and New Zealand. The state is divided into fifty-six counties.

Montana's landscape is varied. The eastern part of the state has high plains, long winding rivers, **badlands**, and isolated mountain ranges. In the west are the rugged Rocky Mountains, scenic valleys, canyons, fast-flowing rivers, alpine lakes, forests, waterfalls, and snow-white glaciers. Above it all is a dramatic view of wide-open sky, earning the state the nickname "Big Sky Country." Montana's more common nickname, however, is "the Treasure State" because, at one time, it produced so much of the country's gold, silver, and copper.

Great Plains

The central and eastern sections of Montana, which make up two-thirds of the state, belong to the region of the United States called the Great Plains. At first glance, the area appears flat and perhaps unremarkable, but the plains are bursting with natural history.

The rolling hills of western Montana turn green in the spring.

For most of the past eight thousand to ten thousand years, native grasses such as buffalo grass, blue grama, and blue bunch wheatgrass covered the plains and fed huge herds of bison. By 1900, however, most of the bison had been killed and farmers began to replace much of the grasslands with planted rows of crops.

During the last Ice Age, which ended about eleven thousand years ago, huge sheets of slow-moving ice called glaciers advanced and receded. As they moved, they carved rugged mountain crest lines, scraped valleys flat, and left behind rocks and debris. As the ice melted, river valleys, potholes, lakes, and wetlands formed. Today, these areas provide rich habitats for red monkey grass and wild asparagus, as well as wild turkeys and ring-necked pheasants.

Central and eastern Montana's two major rivers are the Missouri and the Yellowstone. The Missouri River has its source in southwestern Montana, near Three Forks. It carves a sweeping route north along the foothills of the Rocky Mountains and then flows eastward through the plains. In north-central Montana, at Great Falls, the river drops 500 feet (150 m) in a series of rapids and waterfalls. Farther east, a 149-mile (240 km) stretch of the river has

Montana Borders

North:	Canada
South:	Idaho
	Wyoming
East:	North Dakota
	South Dakota
West:	Idaho

been designated by the US government as the Upper Missouri Wild and Scenic River. This portion of the river flows through spectacular scenery, in an area little touched since American explorers Meriwether Lewis and William Clark visited the region in 1805 and 1806. In this area, called the Missouri Breaks, the river races eastward past rock cliffs, sandstone towers, and ash, juniper, and cottonwood forests.

East of the Breaks, the Fort Peck Dam transforms the Missouri River into a series of long lakes. Fort Peck Lake is one of the largest human-created lakes, or **reservoirs**, in the United States. It is 134 miles (216 km) long and 220 feet (67 m) deep. Surrounding the reservoir is the Charles M. Russell National Wildlife Refuge. This refuge is home to ducks, mule deer, **pronghorns**, elk, bighorn sheep, white-tailed deer, grouse, eagles, and migrating birds.

The Yellowstone River is the longest undammed river in the United States, excluding Alaska. It begins high in the mountains of northern Wyoming and flows into Montana. The river stretches a total of 692 miles (1,114 km) in length. It flows 570 miles (917 km) through Montana. *National Geographic* magazine called it "the last best river."

The Yellowstone is filled with fish such as cutthroat trout, grayling, and paddlefish. Its banks are lined with cottonwood, poplar, and willow forests that provide a habitat for creatures such as bald eagles, red foxes, beavers, otters, and deer. Before the arrival of

The beautiful Yellowstone River got its name from the high, yellow bluffs near Billings, through which it passes.

MONTANA
COUNTY MAP

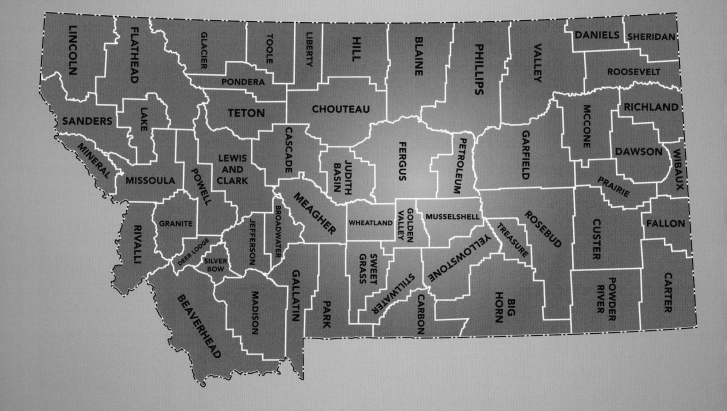

MONTANA

County	Population	County	Population	County	Population
Beaverhead	9,246	Lincoln	19,687	Roosevelt	10,425
Big Horn	12,865	McCone	1,734	Rosebud	9,233
Blaine	6,491	Madison	7,691	Sanders	11,413
Broadwater	5,612	Meagher	1,891	Sheridan	3,384
Carbon	10,078	Mineral	4,223	Silver Bow	34,200
Carter	1,160	Missoula	109,299	Stillwater	9,117
Cascade	81,327	Musselshell	4,538	Sweet Grass	3,651
Chouteau	5,813	Park	15,636	Teton	6,073
Custer	11,699	Petroleum	494	Toole	5,324
Daniels	1,751	Phillips	4,253	Treasure	718
Dawson	8,966	Pondera	6,153	Valley	7,369
Deer Lodge	9,298	Powder River	1,743	Wheatland	2,168
Fallon	2,890	Powell	7,027	Wibaux	1,017
Fergus	11,586	Prairie	1,179	Yellowstone	147,972
Flathead	90,928	Ravalli	40,212		
Gallatin	89,513	Richland	9,746		
Garfield	1,206				
Glacier	13,399				
Golden Valley	884				
Granite	3,079				
Hill	16,096				
Jefferson	11,406				
Judith Basin	2,072				
Lake	28,746				
Lewis and Clark	63,395				
Liberty	2,339				

Source: US Bureau of the Census, 2010

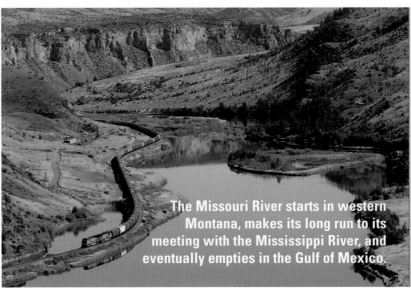

The Missouri River starts in western Montana, makes its long run to its meeting with the Mississippi River, and eventually empties in the Gulf of Mexico.

Granite Peak, the highest point in Montana, is part of the Beartooth Range located in the Absaroka-Beartooth Wilderness.

white settlers, large elk and bison herds roamed the plains near the Yellowstone River. When Lewis and Clark traveled through the area in 1805, they observed many herds of bison crossing the river.

Hundreds of millions of years ago, eastern Montana's plains lay at the bottom of a shallow sea. The land collected rich organic material called sediment. As the sea dried, the sediment turned to rock. Buried in this rock are dinosaur bones, seashells, and other fossils. Water and wind have worn down the rock in many places, leaving dramatic land formations often called badlands. About eighty million years ago, magma surged up from deep within Earth. Magma is extremely hot liquid rock that is called lava once it reaches the surface. As the lava cooled and hardened, it formed mountain ranges in central and eastern Montana. Rising sharply from the flat prairie, these mountains are eye-catching walls of rock with scattered forests of juniper, western larch, and Douglas fir.

The Rocky Mountains

Montana comes from the Spanish word *montaña* for "mountain." The state could not have a better name to describe its western portion. Some seventy to ninety million years ago, a major disturbance occurred deep within the Earth, thrusting rock upward. Volcanoes, glaciers, earthquakes, and other forces of nature went on to shape the mountain chain called the Rocky Mountains.

There are dozens of mountain ranges in Montana's Rocky Mountain region. The state's highest peak—Granite Peak, 12,799 feet (3,901 m) high—rises in the Beartooth Range. Other major ranges include the Anaconda, Bitterroot, Gallatin, Bridger, Madison, Mission, Swan, and Whitefish, as well as the Centennial Mountains.

Montana is also home to seven national forests. These forests have stands of Douglas fir, ponderosa pine, larch, and western hemlock. Wide valleys wind along the base of the mountains. In these valleys, cottonwoods, juniper, white pine, and western cedar grow against a bright backdrop of blue sky.

The crest of the Rocky Mountains creates what is called the Continental, or Great, Divide. This imaginary line runs north–south through the country. East of the Continental Divide, rivers flow toward the Atlantic Ocean and the Gulf of Mexico. West of the Divide, rivers flow toward the Pacific Ocean.

One region in northern Montana is called the Triple Divide. There, water coming down from different mountain peaks heads toward three oceans. Besides flowing east toward the Atlantic and west toward the Pacific, water in this region also drains down off the peaks into Canada and flows northeast to Hudson Bay and into the Arctic Ocean.

Other major rivers in Montana include the Kootenai, Flathead, Blackfoot, Bitterroot, and Clark Fork. All of these rivers eventually flow into the Pacific Ocean by way of the Columbia River. On most of the rivers, dams were built that created lakes. Western Montana has many natural mountain lakes as well. Flathead Lake, the largest natural lake in Montana, is also the largest natural freshwater lake west of the Mississippi River.

Melting snow feeds the Weeping Wall waterfall in Glacier National Park.

Glacier National Park

Grant-Kohrs Ranch

Lewis and Clark Caverns

1. American Computer and Robotics Museum

Visitors to Bozeman's American Computer and Robotics Museum are guided through a timeline that traces the development of the information age. The museum shows how computers were developed and how they changed our lives.

2. Glacier National Park

Located in the northwest corner of the state, Glacier National Park contains pristine forests, alpine meadows, rugged mountains, and spectacular lakes. With over 700 miles (1,127 km) of trails, Glacier is a hiker's paradise.

3. Grant-Kohrs Ranch

Grant-Kohrs Ranch was once the headquarters of a cattle empire that spread over 15,625 square miles (40,469 sq km). Now a **National Historic Site**, it celebrates the role of cattlemen in American history.

4. Kootenai Falls

Located in Kalispell, Kootenai Falls is the largest undammed waterfall in the state. The Kootenai River loses 300 feet (91 m) in elevation traveling a few hundred yards. A swinging bridge is suspended over the river gorge, offering thrills and a breathtaking view.

5. Lewis and Clark Caverns

Located near Cardwell, Lewis and Clark Caverns State Park features one of the largest known limestone caverns in the Northwest. These spectacular caverns, lined with stalactites, stalagmites, columns, and helictites, are naturally cool. They are lighted for a safe visit.

6. Little Bighorn Battlefield National Monument

The Little Bighorn Battlefield National Monument lies south of Billings. This area memorializes the place where 263 soldiers of the US Army's Seventh Cavalry under General Custer died fighting several thousand Native American warriors.

7. Museum of the Rockies

Located in Bozeman, the museum is known for its vast collection of dinosaur fossils. Nicknamed "MOR," the museum also features permanent exhibits on Native American history, a planetarium, and magnificent gardens.

8. Rocky Mountains

Year after year, the scenic spots and recreational activities in Montana's Rocky Mountains attract millions of tourists from all over the world. Whether you enjoy hiking, camping, or extreme mountain sports, Montana's Rocky Mountains provide them all.

9. World Museum of Mining

The World Museum of Mining was founded in 1963 to preserve the rich hard-rock mining history of Butte. The museum is one of the few museums in the world located on an actual mine yard, the Orphan Girl mine.

10. Yellowstone National Park

Established in 1872 as America's first national park, Yellowstone Park is a mountain wildland, home to grizzly bears, wolves, and herds of bison and elk. Old Faithful and the majority of the world's geysers are preserved here.

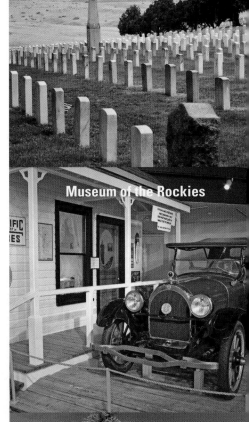

Little Bighorn Battlefield National Monument

Museum of the Rockies

World Museum of Mining

This lake is 27 miles (43 km) long and 16 miles (26 km) at its greatest width, with a maximum depth of 371 feet (113 m).

One lake was actually formed by a naturally created dam. In 1959, a giant earthquake shook loose a wall of rock from a canyon and dammed up the Madison River, creating Earthquake Lake. Today, ospreys and bald eagles make their homes in nearby trees and compete with sport fishermen for so-called Quake Lake trout and whitefish.

Montana's bodies of water also include dazzling waterfalls. As high mountain rivers race down to valleys, crashing walls of water create special habitats for wild trout and river otters. The black swift, a bird that builds its nest behind waterfalls and lays only one egg each year, can be found near many of Montana's waterfalls. Some well-known waterfalls are Palisades, Skalkaho, Natural Bridge, and Kootenai Falls.

Climate

There is nothing dull about the weather in Big Sky Country. In any given year, Montanans can experience snow, hail, **drought**, floods, thunderstorms, Arctic winds, and desert-hot temperatures. The coldest temperature ever recorded in Montana was −70 degrees Fahrenheit (−57 degrees Celsius) at Rogers Pass, north of Helena, in 1954. This is also the record cold temperature for all of the United States except Alaska.

An average of 300 inches (762 cm) of snow falls each year on Whitefish Mountain near Glacier National Park.

Frosty temperatures do not last all winter. Instead, they come in two or three waves of cold spells each year. The average winter temperature around the state is about 10°F (−12°C). Surprisingly warm winds called chinook winds often blow in from the Pacific Ocean. These winds melt snow and take the edge off winter's chill.

In general, summer brings high temperatures, especially in eastern Montana. Summer days can often top 100°F (38°C). The warmest temperature ever recorded in Montana was 117°F (47°C). This occurred at Glendive in 1893 and at Medicine Lake in 1937. But the average summer temperature is 87°F (31°C), and cool winds keep most everyone comfortable.

Throughout the year, the pattern of precipitation is consistent. Clouds filled with moisture from the Pacific move eastward. When they hit the Rocky Mountains, the clouds release their moisture in the form of rain or snow. Once clouds make it over the Rockies into eastern Montana, they have lost much of their moisture.

The average annual precipitation in western Montana is about 20 inches (51 centimeters) of rain or melted snow. In eastern Montana, the average is much less, about 13 inches (33 cm). Droughts with only 6 to 9 inches (15 to 23 cm) of precipitation a year are not unusual. While hundreds of inches of snow can pile up in the Rocky Mountain region, fierce Arctic winds blow so hard across eastern Montana that snow seldom stays long on the ground.

Rapid Change

Glacier National Park's weather can change quickly. Just outside the park's eastern boundary, in 1916 in Browning, Montana, the temperature dropped from 46°F [8°C] to −56°F [−48°C] in twenty-four hours. That is one hundred degrees Fahrenheit in a day! It is still an all-time world record.

Natural Disasters

Earthquakes, slow moving glaciers, storms, and powerful winds helped shape much of Montana's natural beauty, such as mountains, forests, and rivers. These forces of nature have also contributed to the state's severe weather events and other natural disasters. On Montana's Great Plains, warm, moist winds from the Gulf of Mexico flow north while icy Arctic winds travel south. When these two different winds collide, thunder and lightning storms explode overhead, sometimes forming **tornadoes**. Along with violent winds, these storms carry heavy rains that can cause rivers to overflow, flooding homes and farms.

When warm air and cold air collide over Montana, thunderclouds form. Some of these develop into tornadoes.

Lightning strikes sometimes start forest fires and grassland brush fires, which are a part of the natural ecology. Dry conditions can help feed any kind of fire. Large animals such as elk or bear can outrun a fire. Small animals such as prairie dogs or chipmunks seek shelter underground. A burned area is a rich hunting ground for owls and other birds looking for prey. Douglas fir trees have thick bark to protect them from burning. Aspens and cottonwoods have deep roots that quickly sprout new growth after a fire. Lodgepole pines grow a type of cone that will open and let loose its seeds only during extreme heat.

Wildlife

Badgers, coyotes, mule deer, and pronghorns live in eastern Montana. The many lakes, ponds, and wetlands are home to a great variety of fish and amphibians. Trout, perch, bullheads, channel catfish, and paddlefish are just some of the fish swimming through the waters. These bodies of water also serve as important refuges for rare migrating shore birds such as the American white pelican and the great blue heron. Eagles, hawks, wild turkeys, pheasants, grouse, and ducks also live near these watering holes.

When Lewis and Clark reached the Montana plains, they noted numerous prairie-dog "towns." They were charmed by the animal they called the "barking squirrel." But the farmers considered them pests for building mounds and tunnels through farm fields. Ranchers noticed that they disturbed the grasslands where cattle fed. As a result, farmers and ranchers killed off nearly all the prairie dogs. Owls, eagles, and ferrets, creatures that relied on prairie dogs for food, also suffered. The prairie dog is considered a keystone species that plays a major role in the way an **ecosystem** works. An ecosystem is the whole group of living and nonliving things that make up an environment and affect each other.

If a keystone species is removed from an area, the ecosystem would change dramatically or stop existing. To protect the region's prairie dogs, the Montana Department of Agriculture has developed a plan to balance the survival of these animals with the concerns of farmers and ranchers.

Montana is home to many kinds of animals. Mule deer, mountain lions, bobcats, woodpeckers, bats, hawks, and black bears live in the forested mountains and the river valleys of western Montana. Bison live in the National Bison Range Wildlife Refuge. Different types of snakes and lizards can be found throughout the region.

Some of the nation's rarest and most threatened species live in Montana. A species is considered threatened when its numbers are reduced and it is at risk of becoming extinct, or completely dying out. Montana has four threatened animal species—the grizzly bear, Canada lynx, piping plover, and bull trout. It also has three threatened types of plants—the water howellia, Ute ladies' tresses, and Spalding's campion.

Long Journey

The Missouri River is considered to be the longest river in the United States, with a total length of 2,540 miles (4,088 km). The Missouri travels through seven states, starting in Montana.

Some animals that almost vanished have begun to come back. Many of these populations decreased because of overhunting, loss of habitat, or pollution. Laws now prevent fishermen from harming various fish species. Similarly, other animal species, including peregrine falcon, bald eagle, gray wolf, and Rocky Mountain bighorn sheep, are being monitored in the state.

North America's heaviest bird, the trumpeter swan, was nearly driven to extinction in the 1930s by hunters who killed them to provide feathers for women's hats. At one point, there were fewer than two hundred birds remaining, but today, Red Rock Lakes National Wildlife Refuge has thousands.

Montanans are proud of their state and want to preserve both its beauty and its creatures. As one Nez Perce Native American elder explained, "I belong to the land out of which I came. The Earth is my mother."

1. Beaver

Adapted to living both in water and on land, the beaver uses its teeth to cut down trees to dam streams, forming ponds that are a rich habitat for fish, birds, and other creatures. Beavers also build cone-shaped houses called lodges.

2. Bighorn Sheep

Bighorn sheep are at home in Montana's rugged mountains. Their gray-brown coats help them to blend into the mountainside. Bighorn sheep have hooves that are hard with rough soles that provide grip, making them excellent climbers and jumpers.

3. Bison

Also called buffalo, American bison are known for their large size, shoulder humps, and short, dark, and curved horns. Native Americans treasured bison as a source of food and warm skins. Most Montana tribes still keep buffalo.

4. Canada Lynx

The Canada lynx has a thick coat, tufts of fur on its ears, and a short, black-tipped tail. A threatened species in Montana, the lynx hunts at night. It lives in the remote pine and fir forests of Glacier National Park.

5. Common Camas

Early Native American tribes valued the common camas plant so much that the people would battle over ownership of camas fields. This blue-flowered, onion-like plant was harvested for its bulbous roots. Roasted camas roots taste like sweet potatoes.

Bighorn Sheep

Bison

Common Camas

6. Dusky Grouse

The dusky grouse is a handsome bird with a square tail that can fan out. It weighs between 2 and 3 pounds (0.9 and 1.4 kg). It lives in western Montana, staying at higher elevations during winter, and then moving to lower elevations to breed in summer.

7. Grasslands

The Northern Montana Prairies contain some of the largest native grasslands remaining in the United States. Nearly one-fourth of Montana is covered by native grasslands. These rolling hills and river valleys provide critical habitat for birds and animals.

8. Osprey

Ospreys are migratory birds that arrive in Montana in March and April to build their nests. They look for locations near water, which provides safety and food. Ospreys have a diet that consists mainly of fish.

9. Paddlefish

Paddlefish have lived in Montana's rivers for more than three hundred million years. This large fish can grow to a length of 6 feet (1.8 m) and a weight of 120 pounds (54 kg). It resembles a shark but has a long, paddle-shaped snout.

10. Rubber Boa

The rubber boa gets its name from its loose skin, which feels like rubber. It hunts at night, catching and then killing its prey by constricting—or squeezing—the small animal to death. Baby mice are one of its favorite meals.

Grasslands

Paddlefish

Rubber Boa

Tepee rings, which are stones arranged in a circle to hold down the walls of a tepee, are found in the plains of Montana.

From the Beginning

Through prosperous and poor times, glory and sorrow, the people of the Treasure State have struggled and survived. Former US senator Mike Mansfield once said of his home state, "The history of Montana is the song of a people who … have held together, persevered and, at last, taken enduring root."

The First People

The first people who lived in today's Montana were early Native Americans, now known as Paleo-Indians. They are believed to have been descendants of people who crossed a land bridge that once connected Asia and North America more than ten thousand years ago. Over time, they moved south along what are now known as the Rocky Mountains. The route that they followed (along with many other groups of Native Americans who came later) is now referred to as the Great North Trail or the Old North Trail.

Archaeologists (scientists who study past cultures) have found evidence that there was human life in Montana at least seven thousand years ago—and perhaps much earlier than that. These prehistoric people hunted animals such as woolly mammoths and ancient bison. They also gathered plants for food. In time, the climate became very hot and dry,

This rocky cliff was used by Native American hunters as a buffalo jump, which they called a *pishkun*. They drove the animals over these cliffs to their deaths.

and the mammoths and bison moved on. This forced the Paleo-Indians to seek out smaller animals and to rely more on plants growing in river valleys.

About two thousand years ago, the region's climate became cooler, and bison herds flourished again. Native American descendants of the Paleo-Indians followed the herds to hunt them. They used all parts of the animal for food, clothing, tools, fuel, and material for making their homes. These hunters caught their prey by driving the bison herds off high cliffs, known as buffalo jumps. The Native Americans called these buffalo jumps *pishkun*.

Native Americans in the region lived in portable tents called tepees, which were made of bison skins and log poles. To keep a tepee fixed to the ground, the Native Americans held the bison skins down with circular piles of rocks, known as tepee rings. People have found old tepee rings in many areas of Montana, the remains of these early dwellings.

The men of the Plains tribes hunted mostly bison. The Native Americans of the mountains and western valleys hunted deer, trapped small animals, and fished. The women prepared and preserved the meat. They also treated the animal hides for clothing, accessories, and home building. Women of the Plains tribes gathered berries, such as huckleberries. They also dug roots, such as wild carrot, onion, turnip, common camas, and bitterroot.

Exploration

Even though Native Americans and their ancestors had been living on the land for thousands of years, rulers in Europe claimed the region for themselves and their countries during the eighteenth century.

In 1743, two French-Canadian brothers, François and Louis-Joseph Vérendrye, visited the region that includes present-day Montana. They were probably the first Europeans to see the area. Both men worked as fur trappers. They were also explorers looking for a river route to the Pacific Ocean. There is no river route, so after a futile search they returned home.

Although many decades passed without Europeans setting foot again in the region, France still claimed the land as its own. Present-day Montana was part of an area that the French called the Louisiana Territory.

In 1803, France sold the Louisiana Territory to the United States. The deal, called the Louisiana Purchase, doubled the size of the United States. The acquired territory included more than 800,000 square miles (2,000,000 sq km) of land west of the Mississippi River.

Lewis and Clark

Thomas Jefferson, the third US president, had already planned on sending an expedition to explore the region. He had asked his personal secretary, Meriwether Lewis, to lead a

Meriwether Lewis and William Clark entered what is now Montana in April 1805.

The Native People

Native Americans lived in the area we now call Montana long before Europeans arrived. Historians estimate that Native American tribes like the Shoshone and Blackfeet have lived in Montana since at least 1600. The Shoshone came from the south. They were the first people in the area to breed, ride, and trade horses. Their horses were acquired from other Native American groups, who got them from Spanish explorers in the American Southwest during the late sixteenth century.

Other tribes that settled along the west side of the Rocky Mountains were the Flathead, Kootenai, Kalispel, Salish, and Bannock. On the plains, the Crow settled along the Yellowstone River. The Gros Ventres, Assiniboine, Sioux, Chippewa, Cree, and Cheyenne tribes later followed. Native Americans living on the plains during this period were usually nomadic, moving from area to area based on weather and the availability of food. Plains tribes traded with each other but also fought wars. Europeans were surprised by how often the Crow fought with their neighbors, yet how easily they made peace with each other when they were done fighting.

As settlers and miners moved west, Native Americans were forced off their traditional lands. Many Native American groups had to sign agreements, or treaties, with the US government. These treaties granted whites the right to settle on or pass through tribal territory, while Native Americans increasingly were restricted to living on reservations that included only a small portion of their traditional lands. Over the years the US government broke

A young Crow dancer performs at the Crow Fair on the reservation in Montana.

many treaties to make room for even more settlers. Eventually, most Native American rights to the land were taken away.

Today, there are more than sixty-two thousand Native Americans and seven federally recognized tribes living in Montana, making up more than 6 percent of the total population. Most live on one of seven large reservations while others reside in cities like Missoula, Billings, Great Falls, Butte, Helena, and Miles City. Federally recognized tribes have a government-to-government relationship with the United States and are eligible for funding and services from the Bureau of Indian Affairs. They also have certain rights of self-government (tribal sovereignty).

Spotlight on the Crow

In their own language the Crow tribe's name is Apsaalooke (pronounced opp-sah-loh-kay), which means "children of the large-beaked bird." It is also spelled Absarokee or Absaroka. Today, Crow people usually refer to themselves by using the English name, "Crow."

Homes: Like other Plains tribes, the Crow lived in the tall, cone-shaped buffalo-hide houses known as tepees. Since the Crow tribe moved frequently to follow the buffalo herds, a tepee had to be carefully designed to set up and break down quickly, like a modern tent.

Government: Today, the Crow live mostly on a reservation in Montana, which is land that belongs to them and is under their control. The Crow Nation has its own government, laws, police, and services, just like a small country. Crow tribal officers are elected by all the people. However, the Crow are also US citizens and must obey American law.

Clothing: Crow women wore long deerskin dresses. Crow men wore breechcloths with leather leggings and buckskin shirts. Both men and women wore moccasins on their feet.

Language: Nearly all Crow people speak English today, but many also speak their native Crow language. Here are a few easy Crow words: *kaheé* (pronounced similar to "ka-hay") is a friendly greeting, and *ahó* means "thank you."

Food: The Crow were primarily hunting people. Crow men hunted deer, elk, and especially buffalo. Some Crow bands raised corn in their village gardens.

Crafts: Crow artists are famous for their quill embroidery, beadwork, and carving arts.

mission. Lewis in turn asked his army friend, William Clark, to join him. The expedition's four goals were to study the Missouri River, find a water route from the eastern United States to the Pacific Ocean, meet Native peoples, and gather information about plants, animals, landforms, and climate. The two explorers hired a crew, collected supplies, and began to paddle up the Missouri in 1804.

Lewis and Clark spent their first winter in what is now North Dakota. Setting out in the early spring of 1805, the group reached present-day Montana in April. Gazing into the valleys between the Missouri and Yellowstone Rivers, Lewis wrote that he had a "most pleasing view of the country."

Lewis and Clark and their crew—named the Corps of Discovery—faced many challenges in the area. There was no water route through the Rocky Mountains. Traveling overland, they managed to cross the rugged Continental Divide, and they reached the Pacific in November 1805. They wintered near present-day Astoria, Oregon.

During their return trip home in 1806, the group split up for a time to explore more of the region. They were amazed by the mountains, rivers, trees, plains, valleys, plants, and wildlife. Some of the animals they saw included beavers, bison, deer, elk, grizzly bears, and "vast assemblages [groups] of wolves."

At this time in Europe and in the United States, a fashion craze for men's beaver-felt hats was in full swing. On learning that the territory Lewis and Clark had seen was overflowing with beavers, fur trappers began to move into the

Traps were used to hunt beavers for their pelts.

area. In 1807, Manuel Lisa, a Louisiana Spaniard, was the first to set up a trading post in present-day Montana. He established his post near the Bighorn and Yellowstone Rivers.

Pioneers faced many challenges as they traveled west through Montana.

For the next forty years, riverboats, trappers, and traders from fur companies in the East came to the area. American frontiersmen such as Jim Bridger, Jedediah Smith, Kit Carson, and James Beckwourth rose to prominence in the fur business. These so-called mountain men explored much of the West, including present-day Montana.

Wagons West

By the time the demand for beaver-felt hats decreased in the 1840s, most of the beaver population in the region had been wiped out. Many trappers found another line of work—leading wagon trains of pioneers west. Farmers from states east of the Mississippi River had heard tales of the rich, unpopulated land and wanted to claim land for themselves.

Beginning in the early 1840s and continuing for some forty years, hundreds of thousands of families embarked on a four- to six-month journey of about 2,000 miles (3,200 km) to establish themselves on land in the West. The Oregon Trail, which began in Missouri and ended in what was called the Oregon Country of the Pacific Northwest, was one of the first great pioneer trails.

Soon other trails broke off from the Oregon Trail, serving pioneers heading to California and what are now Utah and Colorado. New routes through Montana included the Mullan Road, completed in 1860, and the Bozeman Trail, which opened in 1864. The Mullan Road, the Bozeman Trail, and other routes were used by miners who flooded into the region after gold was discovered, as well as by settlers seeking land to farm. The US government built army forts along the trails to aid and protect the travelers using them.

Making a Compass

When Lewis and Clark explored the western United States, it was important for them to know what direction they were headed. They used a compass to show them north, south, east, and west. The needle on a compass always points toward the North Pole.

It's easy to build your own compass!

What You Need

A sewing needle 1 to 2 inches (2.5 to 5 cm) long

A small bar magnet or refrigerator magnet

A small piece of cork (maybe one from a wine bottle)

A small glass, cup, or bowl of water

Pliers

What To Do

- Rub a magnet over the needle a few times (up to a dozen for weak magnets), always in the same direction. This action magnetizes the needle.

- Cut off a small circle from one end of the cork, about 0.25 inches (6 millimeters) thick. Lay the circle on a flat surface.

- Using a pair of pliers, carefully poke the needle through one edge of the circle. Force the needle through the cork so that the end comes out the other side. Push the needle far enough through the cork so that about the same amount of needle is sticking out each side. Be careful not to stick yourself!

- Fill the glass, cup, or bowl about half full of water, and put the cork and needle assembly on the surface of the water.

- Place your "compass" on a flat surface and watch which way the needle points. It should be north—toward the North Pole!

Striking Gold

In 1858, near Deer Lodge, Montana, brothers James and Granville Stuart discovered gold in a creek bed. Over the next few years, gold was found in Grasshopper Creek near Bannack, at Alder Gulch by Virginia City, and at Last Chance Gulch, now the state capital city, Helena. Once gold was found, thousands of miners flocked to the area, with traders, merchants, farmers, and others close at their heels. They quickly turned the remote mining camps into booming western towns.

When a gold camp was established, there was no federal or state government to create and enforce laws. The rough-and-tumble behavior of many residents made early mining towns in Montana very dangerous. The wild ways of these towns led to a call for order. Many people wanted Montana to become a US territory, a region that was not a state but still had a unified government. US leaders liked the idea, to a large extent because the Civil War (1861–1865) was taking place.

War and Territory

During the Civil War, the Northern states—known as the Union—fought against eleven Southern states, called the Confederacy. The Southern states had left the Union, largely over the issue of slavery. The two sides fought many battles, and hundreds of thousands of people were killed during this bloody war.

Although the conflict took place thousands of miles away, Montana played a role in the war. The Union wanted Montana's gold to help pay for soldiers and supplies. Montana was part of the Idaho Territory that was formed March 4, 1863. Before then, most of the region east of the Rocky Mountains had been part of the Dakota Territory, and the area west of the mountains had been part of the Oregon Territory. An Idaho official, Sidney Edgerton, saw the need for stronger government in the mining towns. In 1863, he traveled to Washington, DC, to lobby for territorial status. The Idaho Territory was divided, and Montana became a new US territory on May 26, 1864. Edgerton was appointed the first governor of the Montana Territory.

Native American Removal

As more settlers moved west, the US government forced Native American tribes to sign agreements, or treaties, that moved them off some of their lands. The Blackfeet tribe did not accept the treaties and often fought bitterly against the US government and white settlers. Other tribes resisted as well.

The Seventh Cavalry was wiped out by a combined force of Sioux and Northern Cheyenne warriors at the Battle of the Little Bighorn in 1876.

In 1876, Sioux and Northern Cheyenne leaders including Sitting Bull, Crazy Horse, Gall, and Lame Deer joined forces. They did not want to give up their land, on which gold had been found. They and their followers left their reservations and waged a series of battles with US Army troops sent to capture or kill them. On June 25, 1876, Lieutenant Colonel George Armstrong Custer and about two hundred soldiers set out to attack a Sioux and Cheyenne encampment near the Little Bighorn River in Montana. More than two thousand Native American fighters surrounded Custer's band of men. Custer and all his men were killed during the Battle of the Little Bighorn.

After this disaster, the US government sought revenge. Congress increased the size of the army and allowed more forts to be built in the region. Large numbers of troops tracked the resisting Native Americans, and either killed them or forced them onto the reservations. The last significant Native American resistance ended in Montana in 1878.

Railroads and Ranches

In the mid-1800s, rough overland trails and riverboats were the only forms of transportation that linked the Montana Territory with the rest of the country. As the territory grew, it needed better methods of transportation. In 1881, the Utah & Northern-

Union Pacific Railroad built a line of tracks to Butte to serve the profitable mining trade. In 1883, the Northern Pacific Railroad laid tracks that connected the northern part of the territory to Portland, Oregon, as well as to Chicago, Illinois, and other cities to the east. The US government granted land to the railroads to encourage them to build lines through the western frontier.

At the same time, cattlemen used Montana's open range for grazing. Many ranchers became wealthy in the 1880s through the 1890s. It was cheap to buy cattle, it cost nothing to feed them, and shipping cattle to markets was easy using the new railroads. More fresh livestock arrived with cowboys who drove herds of longhorn cattle up from Texas. Demand for beef was high, with the increased numbers of city dwellers in the East. And with the coming of the railroads, transportation to the East was readily available. In addition, the confinement of Native Americans to reservations and the shrinking bison herds opened up huge expanses of land. Cities along the rail lines, such as Miles City and Billings, became major livestock centers.

Statehood

Boom times brought people—and wealth—to the Montana Territory, but many Montanans longed for statehood. Statehood would recognize Montana's importance to

The slaughter of the bison opened room in Montana for large herds of cattle.

1. Billings: population 104,170

Billings is Montana's largest city by far, and it's the only one with a population of more than one hundred thousand people. Known as "Montana's Trailhead," Billings offers big-city advantages like restaurants, sports, and access to many outdoor activities.

2. Missoula: population 66,788

Nestled in the Northern Rockies, surrounded by seven wilderness areas, and at the **confluence** of three rivers, Missoula is an outdoor paradise. Missoula is known for its trout fishing and is the home of the University of Montana.

3. Great Falls: population 58,505

Great Falls boasts more than parks and 40 miles (64.4 km) of River's Edge Trail along the scenic Missouri River. It's the home of the Montana State Fair and the state Pro Rodeo Circuit Finals. Nearby is Malmstrom Air Force Base.

4. Bozeman: population 37,280

Bozeman is close to Yellowstone National Park and offers outdoor activities including hiking, fishing, and camping. Bozeman is home to the American Computer Museum and the Museum of the Rockies, as well as Montana State University.

5. Butte-Silver Bow: population 33,525

Montana's first major city began as a gold and silver mining camp and was known as "the richest hill on Earth." Butte is the county seat of Silver Bow County, but they count their population together for the census.

Billings

Great Falls

6. Helena: population 28,190

Montana's state capital, Helena was born when gold was discovered in Last Chance Gulch in 1864. The gulch is now Helena's Main Street and the state's only downtown, outdoor walking mall. Helena's buildings include architectural masterpieces from the late 1800s.

7. Kalispell: population 19,927

Kalispell is located within a thirty-minute drive of Flathead Lake, Whitefish Mountain Ski Resort, Glacier National Park, and several national and state forests. Between 2000 and 2010, the population of Kalispell increased 40 percent as area tourism grew.

8. Havre: population 9,310

Founded as a railroad depot, Havre is located close to the Canadian border. When fire destroyed most of Havre in 1904, business owners moved underground until the town could be rebuilt. You can tour the old underground city.

9. Anaconda: population 9,298

When copper was discovered in nearby Butte in 1882, a smelter was needed to refine the copper **ore**. Anaconda was named for the Anaconda Company, which built its smelter here. When the smelter closed in 1980, the town turned to tourism.

10. Miles City: population 8,410

Located where the Yellowstone and the Tongue Rivers meet, Miles City was founded by merchants who followed the soldiers moving to the area in the 1870s.

Kalispell

Havre Underground

the country and provide full representation in Congress. The state could tax local businesses, and local citizens would be able to elect their own executive and judicial officials.

In 1889, US president Benjamin Harrison signed a law that would give four territories—including Montana—immediate statehood, after each one drafted a constitution. Montanans quickly approved their constitution on October 1, 1889. On November 8, 1889, the president proclaimed Montana the forty-first state in the Union. The people of Montana chose Helena as their state capital over Virginia City and Anaconda by a small margin.

When Copper Was King

Once the Montana gold rush was over, miners discovered other valuable minerals like silver, copper, and lead. Unlike gold, which was found in streambeds and filtered out from the gravel with pans, silver and copper were contained in a hard rock called ore that had to be dug out of mountainsides. Copper and silver miners used heavy machinery to tunnel underground. Smelters, factories that break metal away from ore, were built in Anaconda and Great Falls.

People across the nation were demanding more copper because it was used to manufacture wires for popular new inventions such as the telephone and electric lighting. By 1887, Montana was the nation's largest copper and silver producer.

Hard-rock mining was very expensive. As a result, three wealthy men and their companies soon controlled all the mining operations. William Clark, Marcus Daly, and Fritz Heinze were called the Copper Kings. They competed with each other for power by owning newspapers and influencing judges and members of Congress who made decisions affecting the state.

Two-for-One Deal

Montana cattlemen made a lot of money trading with travelers. As the pioneers with their wagons and livestock trudged along the trail, the ranchers swapped one healthy cow for two worn-out ones. The ranchers would then fatten the cattle on rich Montana grass and drive them south to the Oregon Trail.

All students were educated in this schoolhouse in the mining town of Hecla in the 1890s. Hecla is now a ghost town.

One by one, however, they sold their holdings to Standard Oil, a powerful corporation whose mines were operated by the Anaconda Company, which it owned. People in Butte just called it The Company.

The miners who worked for the Anaconda Company in Butte came from all over the world. Butte became an ethnic melting pot. Miners were Irish, Cornish (from a county in England called Cornwall), Italian, and Chinese, as well as African Americans who came to Montana from other parts of the United States. Miners worked in shifts twenty-four hours a day in the dangerous underground caverns and the noisy, gritty smelters. The mining company controlled almost everything in the miners' lives—the stores where miners shopped, the homes where they lived, and the banks that kept their money.

Workers sometimes felt the company was taking advantage of them, so they formed labor unions. Labor unions are organizations where workers join together to get better pay and working conditions. During the early part of the twentieth century, the Anaconda Company and the labor unions often clashed in violent protests. Such conflicts were reported in newspapers and soon gained national attention.

Homesteading

Farmers had moved into Montana's mining towns during the boom years to feed the new workers. When the mines declined, some workers turned to farming as well. Yet it was not until the beginning of the twentieth century that farmers settled on eastern Montana's plains. In 1862, the federal government had passed the Homestead Act. This law promised 160 acres (65 hectares) of land to any man or woman willing to pay a small filing fee and live and work on land for at least five years. Early homesteaders did not flock to Montana's remote plains until a new law, the Enlarged Homestead Act of 1909, gave new settlers 320 acres (130 ha) of land and lowered the number of years needed to work on it from five to three.

The railroads were also eager to transport more settlers. They placed advertisements in newspapers throughout the East Coast and even in Europe. Some pioneers and **immigrants** were promised "free land." Others paid for their farmland. The railroads also offered cheap rail fares, some including freight and sleeping facilities.

At the beginning of the twentieth century, farmers came from crowded eastern states. They also traveled from more distant European lands, including Sweden, Germany, Poland, Yugoslavia, France, Italy, Spain, Ireland, and Great Britain.

Homesteaders built small cabins because there wasn't a lot of wood in eastern Montana.

Once the newcomers stepped off the train and filed for their land, they quickly had to find shelter and water. That was not easy to do on the dry, treeless plains. They built small houses, put up fences around their fields, dug wells by hand, and hauled water in barrels. Cattle ranchers did not welcome the new settlers, and the two groups argued bitterly about fences and water.

Homesteaders at first were not happy to find the soil so rocky, but they stuck by their claims and discovered that wheat grew well. Within a few years of the beginning of the homestead boom, more than 4,688 square miles (12,142 sq km) of land were being farmed. Towns sprung up around the railroad lines, rains fell, and wheat harvests were plentiful.

Just as the gold rush boom had to end, so did the homestead boom. The United States entered World War I (1914–1918) in 1917, and the federal government asked Montana's farmers to plow as much land as they could to produce food during the war. To speed up production, banks loaned farmers money for new equipment.

Unfortunately, just as farmers started plowing more dirt, a drought hit. After several rainless years, the soil was so dry that it blew away in "black blizzards." Making things worse for farmers, swarms of grasshoppers covered fields and ate crops to the ground. Soon, farmers could not harvest enough wheat to repay their bank loans. Many people lost their farms. By 1925, half of Montana's farmers had "gone bust," and more than half of the region's banks had gone out of business.

Hard Times, a New Deal, and War

While the 1920s were prosperous years for most of the United States, in Montana

Tough Road

The first major overland route through Montana was called the Mullan Road. This wagon road was named after John Mullan, a US Army lieutenant who was ordered to build a trail to link Fort Benton on the upper Missouri River with Fort Walla Walla on the Columbia River in today's eastern Washington.

Senseless Slaughter

Bison were hunted for many reasons. A new tanning method made it more profitable to sell the hides. Railroad companies killed bison to feed their workers and to clear land for the rails. Thrill-seekers joined in the excitement of the hunt. During the 1880s, so many bison were killed that they almost vanished from Montana.

The Public Works Administration paid laborers to build the Fort Peck Dam during the Great Depression.

these years were often filled with despair. Farmers and ranchers could barely make a profit. Droughts set off deadly forest and grass fires that blazed throughout the state. When the price of copper dropped, the Anaconda Company began to shift its business to low-cost mines in Mexico and Chile, leaving many Montana miners out of work. Montana was the only state to decrease in population in the 1920s.

By 1929, the national economy crashed and the entire country was suffering from bank failures and high unemployment. As the 1930s began, people had less money, and they had less use for trains to transport goods. As a result, many of Montana's railway workers, coal miners, and loggers also lost their jobs. This grim period in US history is known as the Great Depression.

Between 1933 and 1939, the thirty-second US president, Franklin D. Roosevelt, created a series of government programs, known as the New Deal, to help residents in all the states. New Deal programs included the Works Progress Administration (WPA), the Public Works Administration (PWA), and the Civilian Conservation Corps (CCC). The

WPA employed people for a wide range of construction and creative projects. The PWA built large projects such as Montana's Fort Peck Dam. The CCC, nicknamed Roosevelt's Tree Army, hired unemployed men to fight forest fires, build forest fire lookout towers, replant trees, and do other useful tasks in forests and other wilderness areas.

By the end of the 1930s, the US government was focusing more on World War II (1939–1945) than on projects at home. The United States entered the conflict in 1941 and fought through the end of the war. In 1942, as part of the war effort, the federal government built two air force bases in Montana—Malmstrom and Glasgow.

Nearly forty thousand Montanans left the state to join the armed forces. Another fifty thousand left to work in West Coast factories, manufacturing products for the war effort. Those at home went back to work growing wheat, raising cattle, logging, and mining.

Montana Today

Montana citizens still live with ups and downs. During the 1980s, the Anaconda Company closed its copper mines in Butte and its smelters in Anaconda and Great Falls, costing thousands of workers their jobs. A new owner bought and updated operations, but modern technology and newer forms of mining meant fewer workers. Copper mining in Montana still exists, although on a diminished level.

Strip mining has been used to uncover coal deposits.

The timber and farming industries have changed as well. Today, logging companies and lumber mills employ fewer workers than in past decades. Farmers and ranchers continue to face challenges due to lower prices for their products as well as spells of dry weather. Most farms in Montana survive today by growing a variety of crops and raising a mixture of livestock.

Coal miners are still at work at the Rosebud Mine near Colstrip in southeastern Montana. Strip-mining began here in 1969. This type of mining involves clearing away the land (and destroying the plant life) that covers a coal deposit. The Rosebud coal-mining operation now includes three active pits.

In 1989, Montana celebrated its statehood centennial. After experiencing slow population growth in the 1980s, the 2010 Census found that the number of Montanans grew by 9.7 percent in the first decade of the twenty-first century, matching the nationwide percentage increase. By 2012, the population exceeded one million state residents for the first time. Natural gas and oil deposits in the northeastern corner of the state, at the Bakken oil field, drew more workers to the state.

Montana has also grown in other ways. Tourism has become a major source for income and jobs in the state. More Americans and people from foreign countries are appreciating the beauty of Montana's wilderness areas and national parks, and the opportunities for outdoor recreation.

Like other states, the years after the nationwide economic downturn that began in late 2007 were hard on Montanans. Yet, despite the state's economic troubles, most Montanans do not want to live anywhere else. Newcomers—many of them technology workers—have come to the state to get away from crowded cities. Some former residents have returned because they appreciate the Treasure State's natural beauty and way of life.

10 KEY DATES IN STATE HISTORY

1. circa 5000 BCE

Prehistoric people hunt bison and mammoths in the region known as present-day Montana.

2. April 30, 1803

The United States purchases the Louisiana Territory from France at a price of $15 million. The purchase doubles the size of the United States and opens the continent to America's westward expansion.

3. April 27, 1805

American explorers Meriwether Lewis and William Clark enter modern-day Montana during their two-year expedition to explore the American west.

4. May 26, 1864

The Montana Territory is formed by an act of Congress and signed into law by President Abraham Lincoln, splitting off Montana's lands from the Idaho Territory.

5. June 25-26, 1876

Sioux and Northern Cheyenne Native Americans defeat troops led by US cavalry officer George Armstrong Custer at the Battle of the Little Bighorn.

6. November 8, 1889

After voters approve a state constitution, Montana becomes the forty-first US state, granting it rights of representation in US government.

7. February 19, 1909

Congress passes the Enlarged Homestead Act, which doubles the amount of land given to new settlers and leads to a homesteading boom in eastern Montana.

8. April 2, 1917

Jeannette Rankin of Montana becomes the first woman to be sworn in as a member of the US Congress. She serves from 1917 to 1919 and again from 1941 to 1943.

9. October 24, 1933

President Franklin D. Roosevelt authorizes construction of the Fort Peck Dam, which creates Fort Peck Lake. It is the highest dam on the Missouri River.

10. January 3, 2012

Governor Brian Schweitzer announces that the state's population has exceeded one million, based on estimates by the US Census Bureau.

Big Sky ski area provides world-class skiing and snowboarding in the winter and miles of biking trails in the summer.

The People

Montanans are fiercely proud to be citizens of their state. Throughout Montana's history, people have come from around the world to settle in this remarkable state and call it home.

People and Places

According to the 2010 US Census, almost one million people lived in Montana. By 2012, the Census Bureau estimated that the state's population had finally passed one million. However, because Montana is so large, it is far from crowded. Statewide, an average of only seven people live in each square mile (2.6 sq km). Compared to other parts of the country, that is very few. New York City, for example, has more than twenty-seven thousand people per square mile. In fact, forty-six of Montana's fifty-six counties are considered "frontier" counties because they have an average population of six or fewer people per square mile.

Only slightly more than one-third of Montanans live in urban areas. The bigger cities and towns are still rather small compared to some other cities in the country. Billings has the highest population, with slightly more than one hundred thousand people. Missoula

These members of the Crow live on one of seven reservations in Montana.

and Great Falls are next in size, with populations of around seventy thousand and sixty thousand, respectively. The next largest cities are Bozeman, Butte, Helena, and Kalispell.

Montana's cities offer residents and visitors many lively events, including Butte's Montana Folk Festival and Missoula's First Night Missoula. The cities also offer unique museums, such as the Museum of the Rockies in Bozeman, and the C. M. Russell Art Museum and the Lewis and Clark National Historic Trail Interpretive Center in Great Falls. The state also has historic parks, art galleries, theaters, and symphony orchestras.

Today in Montana, many small towns are shrinking, especially on the plains in eastern Montana. Young people from farm families move away to attend school or to find jobs. Throughout the plains, deserted homesteads and farms can be seen.

Other parts of the state have seen increasing populations, however. For the past few decades, newcomers have found their way to Montana, hoping to enjoy its special way of life. Most of them settle in the scenic, mountain-ringed valleys of western Montana, such as the Bitterroot, the Gallatin, and the Paradise Valleys.

Native Americans

Native Americans were the first people to settle in Montana. Today, eleven tribal groups, each with its own language and culture but not all federally recognized, live on seven different reservations in the state. The Blackfeet tribe has the most members in Montana, numbering around 9,400. The Crow Reservation and the Fort Peck Reservation, the homeland of Assiniboine and Sioux tribes, are the state's largest. Yet overall, Native Americans make up only about 6 percent of the state's population.

Next to arrive were the trappers who came to Montana to find animal fur to sell back east. Many of the trappers were Roman Catholics from French Canada. They brought with them some Iroquois Native Americans from the East to teach trapping skills to the Native Americans farther west. While working with the Flathead Native Americans, the Iroquois told them about Catholic priests who taught about God and life after death. They called the priests the Black Robes, after their dark-colored religious garments.

The Catholic Influence

Intrigued with these ideas, the Flatheads sent four different groups to St. Louis, Missouri, between 1831 and 1839, to find someone to serve as their priest. The first three groups failed to find anyone, but the fourth was successful. A young Belgian Jesuit named Father Pierre-Jean de Smet agreed to travel back west with the Flatheads. In 1840, he performed a Catholic Mass for the Flatheads in Green River, Wyoming. Then, in 1841, de Smet set

up a religious establishment called St. Mary's Mission in the Bitterroot Valley, near present-day Stevensville, where he taught members of the Flathead tribe how to farm. St. Mary's Mission is believed to be the first permanent white settlement in present-day Montana. Later missionaries built and ran a sawmill and a flour mill there. The mission has been called "Where Montana Began."

Father de Smet recruited others to come to his mission. One man, Italian Jesuit Father Anthony Ravalli, came in 1845. He was not only a priest. Father Ravalli was also the first physician, surgeon, and **pharmacist** in the Montana Territory.

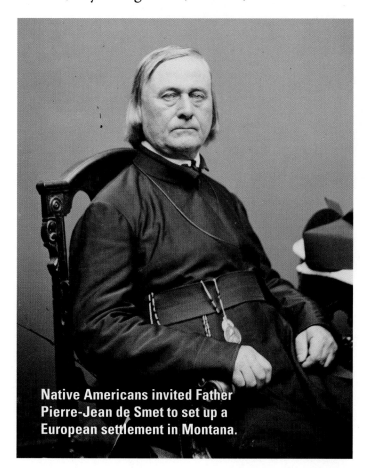
Native Americans invited Father Pierre-Jean de Smet to set up a European settlement in Montana.

Brad Bird

Jesse Tyler Ferguson

Jack Horner

1. Brad Bird

Born Phillip Bradley Bird in Kalispell in 1957, Brad Bird is an American director, animator, producer, actor, and screenwriter. His best known works include *The Incredibles*, for which he directed and wrote the script, *The Simpsons*, *Up*, and *Ratatouille*.

2. Dana Carvey

Dana Carvey, born in Missoula in 1955, spent seven seasons performing on TV's *Saturday Night Live*. He is well known for his comic impersonations of presidents, musicians, and other actors. Carvey has also starred in several movies.

3. Jesse Tyler Ferguson

Born in Missoula in 1975, Jesse Tyler Ferguson is an American actor who starred as Richie Velch in the sitcom *The Class* and is perhaps best known for his role as Mitchell Pritchett on the sitcom *Modern Family*.

4. Jack Horner

Jack Horner is one of the most famous dinosaur researchers in the world. Born in Shelby in 1946, Horner dug for fossils as a child. His discoveries provided evidence that dinosaurs lived in family groups.

5. Chet Huntley

Chet Huntley, a television journalist born in Cardwell, was part of a co-anchor team with David Brinkley for NBC. Among the many honors he earned for his work were eight Emmys he shared with Brinkley and the International Radio and Television Society's Broadcaster of the Year award in 1970.

MONTANA

6. Phil Jackson

Born in 1945 in Deer Lodge, Phil Jackson starred as a player, and has been an outstanding coach and executive in the National Basketball Association (NBA). He has won two NBA titles as a player and eleven as a coach.

7. Evel Knievel

Born Robert Craig Knievel in Butte in 1938, Evel Knievel began performing one-man motorcycle stunts in 1968. Knievel made more than three hundred jumps and broke nearly forty bones. He died in 2007 of natural causes.

8. Christopher Paolini

Born in 1983 in California, Christopher Paolini has lived for most of his life in Paradise Valley, Montana. Famous for writing the international bestsellers *Eragon*, *Eldest*, *Brisingr*, and *Inheritance*, he began writing while in his teens.

9. Charles M. Russell

Born in Missouri in 1864, Charles Russell moved to Montana in 1880 and hoped to become a cowboy. Instead, for the next forty-six years, Russell created more than four thousand paintings and sculptures representing his vision of the West.

10. Michelle Williams

Born in 1980 in Kalispell, Michelle Williams moved to Southern California with her family when she was nine. She began acting as a teenager and landed her first big role at the age of sixteen, in the hit teen show *Dawson's Creek*.

Phil Jackson

Christopher Paolini

Michelle Williams

Who Montanans Are

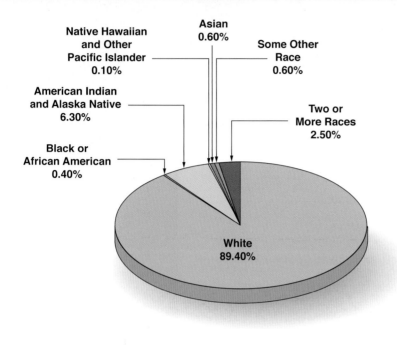

Native Hawaiian and Other Pacific Islander 0.10%

Asian 0.60%

Some Other Race 0.60%

American Indian and Alaska Native 6.30%

Two or More Races 2.50%

Black or African American 0.40%

White 89.40%

Total Population 989,415

Hispanic or Latino (of any race):
- 28,565 (2.9%)

Note: The pie chart shows the racial breakdown of the state's population based on the categories used by the US Bureau of the Census. The Census Bureau reports information for Hispanics or Latinos separately, since they may be of any race. Percentages in the pie chart may not add to 100 because of rounding.

Source: US Bureau of the Census, 2010 Census

A Mix of Cultures

Next to settle in Montana were miners and smelter workers who came from Ireland, Cornwall (in England), Scotland, Finland, Italy, Germany, Eastern Europe, and China, as well as the eastern United States. They settled in cities such as Butte, Anaconda, and Great Falls. To this day, these cities have rich ethnic neighborhoods full of traditional foods and celebrations. Cornish pasties are still considered a signature dish of Butte, for example.

Butte is also known for its large Irish-American population. In the mid-1800s, Irish immigrants were not welcomed by many East Coast communities. As a result, Irish workers moved out west to cities such as Butte for a chance to earn better wages and get a fresh start.

After the miners and factory workers moved to Montana, farmers and ranchers arrived. Many came from states farther east. Others were of Scandinavian, Russian, German, or English heritage. Overall, about 90 percent of Montana's residents today are white European-Americans.

After the Civil War, African Americans moved to Montana to join in the mining boom, but once the boom ended, many left for better jobs elsewhere. Today, approximately 0.6 percent of the population is African American.

New Immigrants

Latino (a person whose family came from South or Central America or Mexico) and Asian immigrants account for a growing and significant share of the population and economy in Montana. The Latino share of Montana's population grew from 1.5 percent in 1990 to 2 percent in 2000, to an estimated 2.9 percent (or 28,565 people) in 2010. After the Vietnam War ended in the 1970s, many Southeast Asian immigrants moved to the state, mainly forming communities in the Bitterroot Valley. Asian Americans made up 0.6 percent of the state population (or 6,253 people) in 2010, according to the US Census Bureau.

Immigrants (the foreign-born) now make up 2 percent of the state's population, and almost half of them are naturalized US citizens who are eligible to vote. Immigrants are not only important to the state's economy as workers; they also account for tens of millions of dollars in tax revenue and consumer purchasing power. Moreover, Latinos and Asians (both foreign-born and native-born) wield $973 million in consumer purchasing power, and the businesses they own had sales and receipts of more than $300 million and employed more than four thousand people at last count.

Many Faiths

A number of different religious faiths are practiced in Montana, a reflection of the state's ethnic diversity. Many Montanans are Roman Catholic, the most common faith of Irish and Italian immigrants in the nineteenth century. Many other Montanans follow the Lutheran faith, introduced by German and Scandinavian farm families. There are many followers of various other Protestant faiths, as well as members of the Church of Jesus Christ of Latter-day Saints—also called Mormons.

Some Montanans follow the Hutterite faith. More than a century ago, Hutterite farmers from Russia and Germany settled the plains and valleys of Montana. Today, there are thirty-nine Hutterite communities. Hutterite families live together on large farms and ranches, where they produce most of the state's pork and much of its eggs and milk. They share their property and income, and they dress similarly. Men wear black pants, hats, and jackets, and women wear long dresses, vests, and scarves. Although Hutterites use modern farm machinery, as part of keeping their faith,

Not Much Change

Virginia City was founded in 1863 and is considered to be the most complete original town of its kind in the United States.

they avoid such worldly goods as cars and electronic products.

Education

Education is very important to Montanans. Taxpayers do their best to provide a good education to all students, whether they live in a city or in a rural area. Schools in small towns are important hubs for community activities, from youth sports such as basketball and football to public meetings or cultural events such as concerts and plays.

The campus at Missoula is the largest of the four in the University of Montana system.

Montana has two large public university systems—Montana State University and the University of Montana. Montana State University has campuses in Billings, Bozeman, and Havre, as well as the College of Technology in Great Falls. The University of Montana's main campus is in Missoula. Three additional campuses are located in Butte, Helena, and Dillon. Students can also attend various community and private colleges.

Each Native American reservation has its own college, run by the tribes. Dr. Joe McDonald helped create Salish Kootenai College on the Flathead Reservation and served as its president for three decades. He is also the founder of the nationwide American Indian College Fund, which raises money for Native American students. "Family is all important to us, and we try to match the school to the community—kind of like a spider on a mirror. Arts, music, and the lore of the Crow Nation are at the heart of our program," said Dr. Janine Pease, former president of Little Big Horn College on the Crow Reservation.

In 2005, the Montana legislature provided funding for public schools to teach all Montana schoolchildren about their state's Native American cultures. The focus on various tribes has helped Native American students feel proud of their distinct and rich heritage.

Sports in Montana

Montana has no major league sports teams. Four Montana teams play minor-league baseball in the Pioneer League. The state's minor league baseball fans support the Billings Mustangs, the Great Falls Voyagers, the Helena Brewers, and the Missoula Osprey.

In college sports, both the University of Montana Grizzlies and the Montana State University Bobcats compete in the Big Sky Conference. The University of Montana offers fifteen intercollegiate men's and women's sports programs. Montana State University has thirteen programs, including men's and women's ski, tennis, basketball, and cross-country teams.

Living In and Visiting Montana

Montana is the place to be if you love the outdoors. The state has many streams for fishing, rivers for rafting, and wilderness areas for hiking, horseback riding, rock climbing, and hunting. Residents and tourists like to swim, boat, and visit the state's national parks. A favorite event in July is the Governor's Cup Walleye Tournament, in which fishers from all over the West compete for the biggest walleye in Fort Peck Lake. In the winter, there is powdery snow for skiing, snowboarding, and snowmobiling. Ski slopes and backcountry trails are full of Montanans and others enjoying a winter's day.

Around the state, there are festivals of all kinds, honoring ethnic heritage, western history, and religious holidays. Each year, the Chippewa and Cree tribes host the Rocky Boy Powwow. The event celebrates Native American heritage and culture. In August, the Crow Fair is an annual gathering open to the public, and many say that the fair has the largest gathering of tepees anywhere.

The town of Libby celebrates its logging past with food and entertainment during Libby Logger Days. The German harvest celebration Oktoberfest fills the streets of Anaconda each year with traditional dance, music, and food. Billings honors Mexican-American culture in an Annual Mexican Fiesta in July.

There are other ways Montanans enjoy their state. There are kayak races, battlefield reenactments, rodeos, and more. One special event is the Festival of Nations, held in the former mining town of Red Lodge, where the community pays tribute to the people who settled the area. Visitors enjoy ethnic foods, foreign movies, Irish fiddlers, Italian and Native American dancers, Scandinavian children's dancers, Slavic pig roasts, and a parade honoring people of all nations. This community event shows the close-knit spirit of Montanans.

10 KEY EVENTS

Annual Bison Roundup

Custer's Last Stand Reenactment

1. Annual Bison Roundup

In October, visitors to the National Bison Range Wildlife Refuge in Moiese can watch rangers herd snorting, stampeding bison into sturdy corrals. After checking on their health, the rangers auction some to ranchers and donate others to tribes.

2. Custer's Last Stand Reenactment and Little Big Horn Days

Every June, hundreds of re-enactors gather near the site of the Battle of the Little Bighorn to relive the event sometimes called Custer's Last Stand, part of a four-day festival held in Hardin.

3. Great Montana Sheep Drive

Every September in Reed Point, hundreds of sheep charge down Reed Point's Main Street to the delight of spectators. A parade and dance add more fun to the event.

4. Lewis and Clark Festival

Two historic sites on Lewis and Clark's route are located near Cut Bank—Camp Disappointment and the Two Medicine Fight Site. Cut Bank citizens hold a festival every July to honor the explorers and the Corps of Discovery.

5. Montana Folk Festival

Every year in July, this three-day festival is held in Butte, against the backdrop of this historic town. It draws the finest traditional musicians from Montana and around the country, who perform on multiple stages. It was started in 2011 after the National Folk Festival ended a three-year run in Butte.

6. Montana State Fair

In late July and early August, Montanans pour into the Montana Expo Park near Great Falls to celebrate their shared culture and history. There are carnival rides, livestock shows, horse races, lumberjack contests, arts and crafts, and food.

7. North American Indian Days Celebration

Montana's largest tribe, the Blackfeet, hosts a celebration and powwow in July on the Blackfeet Reservation fairgrounds in Browning. Visitors enjoy traditional costumes and dress, Native American dance and drumming competitions, stick games, food, rodeos, and races.

8. Race to the Sky

Every February since 1986, dozens of **mushers** and their dogs compete in this sled-dog race through parts of the Rocky Mountains. Winners of the 300-mile (483-kilometer) competition have gone on to win the Iditarod sled-dog race across Alaska.

9. Wolf Point Wild Horse Stampede

This three-day celebration includes a rodeo that brings the best cowboys to town. There is a parade each day, along with a carnival, the Human Stampede Run/Walk, the world-famous wild horse race, a kids' stick-horse rodeo, and street dances.

10. Yellowstone River Boat Float

People from all over the country gather on the second weekend in July to float on the beautiful Yellowstone River, retracing part of the route of the Lewis and Clark Expedition.

Montana State Fair

Race to the Sky

A cowboy and a Native American chief are two of the four circular paintings that can be seen in the rotunda at the state capitol in Helena.

How the Government Works

F rom the time that Lewis and Clark explored the West through the years before Montana became a territory in 1864, many of the region's trappers, miners, and adventurers had little use for an orderly government. As more people arrived, an organized set of rules was needed. In 1864, citizen lawmakers gathered to write more than seven hundred pages of laws for the new Montana Territory. Twenty-five years later, lawmakers drafted a state constitution, and Montana became the forty-first state on November 8, 1889.

Powerful business leaders influenced many rules written into the first constitution and the laws passed in the early years of statehood. Soon, however, citizens began to demand new laws and changes, or amendments, to their constitution. Montanans gave women the right to vote in 1914. They also passed laws that protected workers and children, and it was one of the first states to adopt the lawmaking methods of initiative and referendum. In an initiative, citizens can suggest a law, and if enough people vote in favor of the proposal in an election, then it becomes a law without having to be approved by the state legislature. In a referendum, citizens can vote to have an existing law changed or removed.

By the late 1960s, Montanans had added forty-one amendments to their constitution. Voters decided that was too many and asked lawmakers to write a new constitution.

Ratified in 1972, the new constitution has some of the most progressive provisions in the nation. Citizens are guaranteed rights to individual privacy and open meetings. The constitution affirms a right to clean air and water. Montana's 1972 constitution was also the first state constitution that recognizes and promises to preserve the "unique cultural heritage of the Native Americans."

The state of Montana is represented at the federal level in Washington, DC, by two US senators and one representative in the US House of Representatives.

From Local to State

Montana's fifty-six counties are made up of cities and towns. Nearly every city or town in Montana has its own local government. The cities or towns may be run by a manager, a mayor, selectmen, or a town or city council. These governmental bodies manage local budgets, public schools, land use, and other zoning concerns.

The state is also divided into districts. These districts have elected officials who represent them in the state government. Redistricting takes place every ten years to ensure that all districts have populations of similar size.

The state government passes laws and adopts policies on issues that affect the whole state. State government responsibilities include setting statewide education policies,

The state of Montana acquired this mansion in 1913 to serve as its first residence for the governor.

maintaining law and order, providing emergency services, and overseeing basic services such as transportation, communication, and water.

Branches of Government

The state government has three branches—executive, legislative, and judicial.

Executive

The chief officer of the executive branch is the governor. He or she is elected to a four-year term. Generally, a person may not serve as governor for more than eight years in any sixteen-year period. However, an official can be reelected by a write-in vote, even if he or she has already served eight years. The governor's duties include proposing new laws and appointing important officials. He or she must also sign bills into law or reject (veto) them.

The lieutenant governor, secretary of state, attorney general, auditor, and superintendent of public schools are other key members of the executive branch. Like the governor, they serve four-year terms.

Legislative

The legislature has two chambers, the Montana State Senate and the House of Representatives. The senate is made up of fifty state senators, and the house has one hundred state representatives. Senators hold office for four years, and elections take place for half of the senate every two years.

Representatives hold office for two years. An individual may serve in either chamber for eight years of any sixteen-year period. Members of the legislature meet every other year for ninety days, unless a special session is called.

Judicial

The judicial branch is a system of courts made up of a Supreme Court, district courts, and lower courts. The Supreme Court is the highest court in the state and oversees all other courts. Decisions of lower courts can be appealed to the Supreme Court, which can approve or change them. The Supreme Court can also rule on whether a state law agrees with or violates the state constitution. The Supreme Court has a chief justice and six associate justices. They are elected to eight-year terms. District courts are trial courts. District judges are elected to six-year terms. Lower courts, such as city courts and justices of the peace, rule on small claims and traffic violations. There is also a water court and a workers' compensation court.

Legislators discuss and vote on bills in the state capitol.

How a Bill Becomes a Law

Although voters can create new laws through the initiative process, most new laws are created by the state legislature. A proposed law, or bill, usually begins in either the senate or the house of representatives (except for bills involving spending money from the state budget, which must originate in the house). Only a member of the legislature can introduce a bill.

A legislator who has an idea for a bill asks the legislative staff to write a draft of the bill. The bill is read to the chamber that the legislator is a member of (either the senate or the house). Then, it is sent to the appropriate committee of that chamber for consideration. A bill about farming, for example, is sent to the Agriculture Committee. Every legislator serves on at least one committee.

The relevant committee holds a public hearing for citizens to share their views about the bill. The committee then votes to approve the bill—as is or with changes—or to reject it. A rejected bill goes no further, or "dies" in committee. Sometimes a committee will "table" a bill, or take no action on it. A tabled bill also usually dies in committee.

A bill approved in committee goes back to the chamber where it started for a second reading. During this reading, the bill is debated and possibly changed, and members vote on it. If passed, the bill moves to a third reading, and another vote is taken. If the bill passes by a majority vote after the third reading, it is sent to the other chamber of

Tribal governments meet and pass laws on each of the seven Native American reservations in Montana.

the legislature. There, it goes through the same process of committee and perhaps full-chamber consideration.

Sometimes, the second chamber makes changes to a bill before passing it. If the two chambers pass different versions of a bill, a conference committee, with members from both chambers, is usually appointed to work out a compromise between the house and senate versions. This compromise then has to be approved by both chambers.

A bill that passes in both the house and the senate in the same form then is sent to the governor. The governor can sign the bill into law, veto the bill, or take no action. If the governor takes no action, the bill becomes law in ten days. If the governor vetoes a bill, sometimes it never becomes law. However, the legislature can override the veto. If both chambers again vote in favor of the bill—by a two-thirds majority in each chamber—the bill becomes law despite the governor's disapproval.

Tribal Governments

Each of the seven Native American reservations in Montana has its own government. Each government manages schools, businesses, and natural resources on the reservation. Residents of each reservation elect a council and a chairperson to head the government. Reservation governments collect their own taxes and run their own police and court systems.

POLITICAL FIGURES
FROM MONTANA

★ Denise Juneau: Superintendant of Public Instruction, 2009-2017

Denise Juneau was elected in 2008 and reelected in 2012 to head the agency that runs Montana's schools. She cannot seek a third straight term. A member of the Mandan and Hidatsa tribes, Juneau is the first Native American woman elected to a statewide position. Juneau grew up in Browning.

★ Michael "Mike" Mansfield: US Senator, 1953-1977

Born in New York in 1903, Mike Mansfield moved to Montana as a child. After joining the navy and working in a copper mine, Mansfield served five terms as a US representative, four terms as a US senator, and ten years as US ambassador to Japan. As Senate majority leader, he pushed through civil rights legislation.

★ Jeannette Rankin: US Representative, 1917-1919, 1941-1943

Jeannette Rankin was born near Missoula in 1880. She campaigned for women's voting rights in Montana, which passed in 1914. In 1916, she became the first woman elected to Congress. She was the only congressperson to vote against our entry into World War II.

MONTANA
YOU CAN MAKE A DIFFERENCE

Contacting Lawmakers

To find contact information for Montana legislators, go to this website:

leg.mt.gov/css/find%20a%20legislator.asp.

You can search for legislators and their contact information by name, address, or district. If you don't know which district you live in, click on the link under address, then type in your address. To find contact information for Montana's US congressmen, visit:

mt.gov/govt/congressional_delegation.mcpx

Helping Kids to Cope

In the state with the worst suicide rate in the nation, Montana now has a law aimed at helping to curb suicide among young people. From 1994 through 2013, Butte-Silver Bow, Montana, experienced 189 suicides in their community. The Butte-Silver Bow Suicide Prevention Committee was formed in early January 2014 by county chief executive Matt Vincent after a child died by suicide earlier that month. It was the third youth suicide in the community over a six-week period.

The committee began to work with the Montana state legislature to pass a law that would develop suicide awareness and prevention programs for schools in Montana. Employees would be encouraged to complete two hours of training every five years. A bill was introduced in the house on February 2, 2015. It was passed by the house on February 18 and by the senate on April 15.

In a room filled with Butte High Career Center students, Suicide Prevention Coalition members, and bill sponsor Representative Edie McClafferty, Governor Steve Bullock signed House Bill 374 into law at the Butte-Silver Bow Health Department on May 12, 2015. The law required the Office of Public Instruction to develop a suicide prevention curriculum statewide for teachers and staff.

North-central Montana has soil that
is perfect for growing wheat.

Making a Living

"**E**verything comes from the land, water, sun, or air," said Montana historian Joseph Kinsey Howard. "They are natural elements owned in common by all and not worth anything in terms of money. If everything is made of land, air, water, and sun, where does it get its value? From labor."

Making a living in Montana has never been easy. Citizens have often had to rebuild after a drought, a storm, or a fire, and start all over again. Throughout their history, Montanans have proudly worked with—and against—the elements.

Farming and Ranching

In a state where cattle outnumber people, agriculture remains the backbone of Montana's economy. Montana's ranches and farms provide a wide variety of products, from crops to beef to wool, which stand out as some of the highest quality and most highly desired throughout the United States and the world.

The plains region of north-central Montana, known as the Golden Triangle, has rich, black soil and produces the state's best wheat and barley. Ranches raise cattle, hogs, sheep, llamas, and horses. Together, cattle and wheat make up about 70 percent of the state's total income from agriculture. The agriculture industry brought Montana more than $4.2 billion in 2012.

Sheep produce millions of pounds of wool on the farms of Montana, such as this one near Hilger.

Of the more than twenty-nine thousand farms and ranches in the state, most are family-run. A farm typically grows crops, and a ranch raises livestock. Farms and ranches that do both tend to be the most successful. Nearly 95,300 square miles (247,000 sq km) of land is used for farms or ranches, and Montana ranks second in the nation in the amount of agricultural land. The average size of a farm or ranch in Montana is a little more than 2,000 acres (809 ha) or about 3.1 square miles (8 sq km). Ranches, especially in eastern counties, are generally larger, in order to provide enough grazing land for their animals. Farms are somewhat smaller.

In some western valleys, the number of farms is decreasing. Periods of drought or low prices make it increasingly hard for farmers to pay their bills. Newcomers who move to the area to retire or to escape busier lifestyles are looking for scenic farmland on which to build their houses. During hard times, farmers see this as a way to make money. They divide their big farms into 20- to 40-acre (8 to 16 ha) plots of land, called ranchettes, and sell off the plots. As farms are broken up and sold, many citizens worry about losing an important part of their state's history and culture.

Mining

Gold was the first important mineral found in the rich hills and valleys of the state. Silver and copper were discovered later. Today, gold, silver, and copper are still mined, but not as much as they once were. Luckily, other minerals have risen up to take their place, including lead, zinc, and rare metals like platinum and **palladium**. Platinum and palladium are used in jewelry, dentistry, pharmaceutical drugs, chemical products, and electronics. Montana is also one of the major producers of talc in the United States. Other minerals mined in the state include sand and gravel

Montana also contains deposits of minerals used for fuel, such as coal, petroleum, and natural gas. Settlers first used coal for heating. Later, the railroads used it to power trains. Today, near the town of Colstrip, huge mining operations pull coal from the ground and use it to fuel four large coal-burning electrical generators. The electricity is sold to other states. Coal-fired power plants are also located in Billings. Oil and natural gas are produced from rich deposits in the plains of eastern Montana. Underground pipelines carry the oil and gas to refineries.

Present-day mining techniques now use machinery to replace tasks that were once done by people, which means fewer jobs for workers. However, problems left over from mining operations in the past have helped to create new jobs in old mining towns like Anaconda and Butte. For example, the Anaconda smelter site and the abandoned open-pit mines near Butte have left behind hazardous wastes. One serious situation is the Berkeley Pit above the town of Butte. This polluted hole is filled with water that could spill over into nearby streams and drinking water sources. Scientists and other skilled workers have built water treatment plants and other facilities to help protect the city and the environment from this danger. Efforts to clean up the Berkeley Pit have created jobs for many people in Butte.

Forest Products

Forests cover nearly one-quarter of Montana—about 35,150 square miles (91,038 sq km). The timber industry, or the business of cutting trees and preparing them for use, started in the early days of white settlement. Today, most of the state's forest products are shipped out of state for use in building homes and furniture. Wood from Montana's forests is also processed into paper, plywood, construction materials, and telephone poles.

In 2013, about seven thousand of the more than twenty-two thousand total manufacturing jobs in Montana came from the forest products industry. The manufacturing of wood products ranked first in the manufacturing sector in Montana in terms of jobs, contributing significantly to the state's economy.

The timber industry has been hurt in the past by forest fires in Montana. In 2000, nearly 938 square miles (2,429 sq km) of forest burned in the state. Fires began in

Cattle

Coal

1. Cattle

Cattle make up the largest portion of livestock in Montana. The state has more than 2.5 million head of beef cattle. That means there are about three head of cattle for every human in the state. Montana also has eighteen thousand dairy cows.

2. Coal

Montana was the seventh-largest producer of coal in the United States in 2013. Most of the mines are strip mines located on federal or tribal lands. Coal is used to generate electricity that is sold to other states.

3. Food Processing

Food manufacturing is one of the fastest growing sectors in Montana. Montana is a leading producer of certified organic wheat and is home to a multimillion-dollar honey and pollinating industry. Other products include cereal, candies, jams, pasta, and wine.

4. Handcrafted Log Homes

Montana is a leading producer of log homes. These energy-efficient homes are made from western red cedar or pine. Many builders use dead or burned trees instead of cutting living timber. Most log homes are delivered out-of-state.

5. Mining

In 2012, the mining industry provided 22,750 jobs statewide. Mining jobs in Montana are high paying—96 percent higher than the average wage in the state. Montana mining operations created more than $1.6 billion worth of mineral, metal, and fuel products.

MONTANA

6. Missiles

Located at the eastern edge of Great Falls, the Malmstrom Air Force Base encompasses 5.5 square miles (14.24 sq km). Military technicians care for 150 Minuteman III intercontinental ballistic **missiles** as part of the nation's military defense.

7. Real Estate

The real estate industry continues to grow in Montana. In 2012, real estate contributed more than $6.7 billion to the Montana economy, accounting for nearly 17 percent of the state's total. The industry includes home construction, real estate sales, rentals, and other related services.

8. Sheep

Farmers first brought sheep to Montana during the mining boom. When miners preferred eating beef over mutton (meat from sheep), sheep farmers turned to producing wool products. Today, Montana produces more than 2 million pounds (907,184 kg) of wool each year.

9. Tourism

Tourism is the state's fastest-growing industry. Nearly eleven million visitors spent nearly $4 billion in 2014 at attractions such as historic sites, trout-fishing streams, national parks, ski slopes, and guest ranches. Tourism and recreation businesses support more than forty-two thousand jobs in Montana.

10. Wheat

Montana's farmers produce hard wheat and durum. The state is third among the top wheat-producing states in the country.

Sheep

Tourism

Recipe for Montana Honey-Berry Popsicles

Montana has a wide variety of berries, including huckleberries, blackberries, raspberries, and strawberries. Native Americans once used huckleberries for food, drink, and dyes.

You can use a variety of berries to make delicious frozen popsicles.

What You Need

6 cups (1.5 liters) of Montana huckleberries, blackberries, and raspberries (2 cups or 500 milliliters of each variety)

¾ cup (177 mL) honey, divided

Twelve 3-ounce (90 mL) paper cups or popsicle molds

Twelve popsicle sticks

What To Do

- In a blender or food processor, puree the berries with the honey.
- Divide the mixture evenly between the twelve cups or molds.
- Insert one popsicle stick in each cup or mold.
- Freeze until firm, about thirty minutes.

For an interesting twist, you can mix the berries separately and either freeze 2 cups (500 mL) of each type or layer the flavors in the popsicles.

- Rinse the blender or food processor in between blending each kind of berry.
- To layer, add the first layer, filling the cup of mold a third of the way, and put in the freezer until frozen.
- When the first layer is firm, add another puree into molds and insert a popsicle stick, and add the third and final layer. Freeze until firm.

More than 32,000 acres (13,000 ha) of timber burned in the Red Eagle wildfire in 2006.

June and continued through mid-September. Nearly half of the area burned was in the Bitterroot National Forest. A Bitterroot Valley resident said, "It was awful. We watched elk come out of the hills, and they were steaming!" The fire brought communities together to talk about the best way to combat forest fires in the future.

Renewable Energy

Montanans use about one-half of the electricity generated in the state. The rest is sent to other western states by high-voltage **transmission lines**. Generating more electricity for sale in other states is seen as an economic opportunity for Montana, but existing transmission lines are congested, and new capacity must be built in order to expand sales.

Montana boasts substantial renewable energy resources. Renewable energy comes from sources like wind, running water, and the sun that occur naturally and replace themselves. Montana's mountainous terrain along the Continental Divide creates fast-running rivers that are used by **hydroelectric** dams to create power. Six of the state's ten largest generating plants are hydroelectric facilities, and Montana is a major hydroelectric power producer.

Another resource of Montana's open plains is wind. Montana owns some of the best commercial wind potential in the nation. In recent years, wind turbines have been set up

Kerr Dam on the Flathead River produces hydroelectric power.

to convert the power of wind into electricity. Montana has built several large-scale wind farms in the center of the state, and more are in various stages of planning. Wind electric power generation in Montana grew by almost 32 percent in 2013 and supplied 6 percent of the state's total electricity.

Manufacturing

Manufacturing is one of the smaller industries in Montana. Meatpacking, flour milling, and sugar refining are the state's major food-processing operations. The manufacture of plywood and paper products is part of the timber industry. There are petroleum refineries in Billings, Great Falls, and Laurel. An aluminum plant is located in Columbia Falls.

At Your Service

Service jobs, such as careers in health care, are a fast-growing part of Montana's economy. Colleges and universities provide education, research, and clerical jobs. There are also employment opportunities in government, transportation, publishing, and printing. Other service jobs are in banking, insurance, law enforcement, social services, retail sales, and tourism.

Seeing the Beauty

The tourism industry produces the second-highest amount of income for the state, after agriculture. Montana tourism brought in more than $4 billion in 2014. Montana is home

The Bob Marshall Wilderness is a haven for hikers.

to some of the most popular natural wonders in the world. On March 1, 1872, President Ulysses S. Grant set aside 3,440 square miles (8,910 sq km) of wilderness in the western United States for "the benefit and enjoyment of the people." Yellowstone National Park, a portion of which is located along part of Montana's southern border, was the country's first national park.

Northwestern Montana is home to Glacier National Park. Established in 1910, the park is the most-visited place in Montana. One of the largest glaciers in the park is Grasshopper Glacier. Here, millions of extinct, prehistoric grasshoppers are frozen in the ice.

National wilderness areas are wild places where nature is left untouched by humans. The largest national wilderness in Montana is the Bob Marshall Wilderness Area. It is named after an American environmentalist who in 1935 cofounded the Wilderness Society, an organization that works to protect wild places. Located in northwestern Montana, the Bob Marshall Wilderness straddles the Continental Divide. Montanans fondly call this special place "The Bob."

People come to Montana to enjoy the great outdoors. More than eleven million tourists visit its ski resorts, guest ranches, remarkable national parks, and other attractions each year. There are many ways to appreciate the Treasure State.

MONTANA
STATE MAP

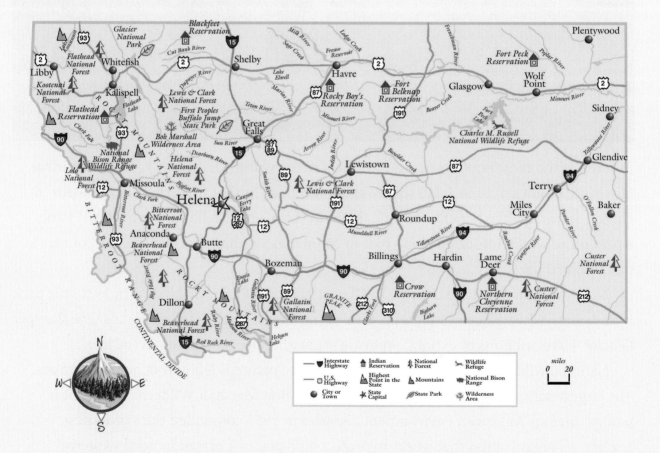

Plentywood

Kootenai
Glacier National Park
Flathead National Forest
Whitefish
Libby
Kootenai National Forest
Kalispell
Flathead Reservation
National Bison Range Wildlife Refuge
Lolo National Forest
Missoula

Blackfeet Reservation
Cut Bank River
Shelby
Lewis & Clark National Forest
First Peoples Buffalo Jump State Park
Bob Marshall Wilderness Area
Helena National Forest
Great Falls

Milk River
Sage Creek
Fresno Reservoir
Ledge Creek
Havre
Rocky Boy's Reservation
Fort Belknap Reservation

Fort Peck Reservation
Poplar River
Wolf Point
Glasgow
Missouri River
Sidney

Charles M. Russell National Wildlife Refuge
Glendive
Terry

Lewistown
Lewis & Clark National Forest
Helena
Canyon Ferry Lake
Miles City
Baker
Custer National Forest

Bitterroot National Forest
Anaconda
Beaverhead National Forest
Butte
Bozeman
Roundup
Billings
Hardin
Lame Deer
Northern Cheyenne Reservation
Custer National Forest

Dillon
Beaverhead National Forest
Gallatin National Forest
GRANITE PEAK
Crow Reservation
Bighorn Lake

ROCKY MOUNTAINS
BITTERROOT RANGE
CONTINENTAL DIVIDE

Clark Fork
Flathead Lake
Dupuyer River
Teton River
Marias River
Sun River
Dearborn River
Bigfoot River
Smith River
Judith River
Arrow River
Musselshell River
Yellowstone River
Boulder Creek
Beaver Creek
Fort Peck Lake
Ferhman River
Musselshell River
Rosebud Creek
Tongue River
Powder River
O'Fallon Creek
Clarks Fork
Bighorn Lake
Red Rock River
Madison River
Ruby River
Big Hole River
Bitterroot River
Gallatin River
Ennis Lake
Hebgen Lake
Lake Elwell

N
W   E
S

Legend

Interstate Highway	
U.S. Highway	
City or Town	
Indian Reservation	
Highest Point in the State	
State Capital	
National Forest	
Mountains	
State Park	
Wildlife Refuge	
National Bison Range	
Wilderness Area	

miles
0   20

MONTANA
MAP SKILLS

1. What mountain range lies closest to the Continental Divide?

2. What is Montana's state capital.

3. What is the highest point in Montana?

4. What Native American reservation can be found just east of Glacier National Park?

5. If you started at the city of Libby in the northwest part of Montana, what US highway could you take to go east and cross the entire state?

6. The cities of Sidney, Glendive, Terry, Miles City, and Billings all are located by which river?

7. What national forest is located close to Lewistown?

8. Interstate highways 90 and 94 meet at which Montana city?

9. What lake lies just south of Glasgow?

10. The city of Plentywood is located in which corner of the state: Northeast, Northwest, Southeast or Southwest?

Granite Peak

Fort Peck Lake

10. Northeast
9. Fort Peck Lake
8. Billings
7. Lewis & Clark National Forest
6. Yellowstone River
5. US Route 2
4. Blackfeet Reservation
3. Granite Peak
2. Helena
1. Bitterroot Range

State Flag, Seal, and Song

The Montana state flag is easy to spot. Large gold letters spell out "Montana" at the top of the dark blue flag. In the center, below the letters, is the state seal, which displays some of the state's beautiful scenery and reflects some pioneer activities, including mining and farming. A brilliant sun rises behind mountains, forests, and the Great Falls of the Missouri. The Montana flag was first adopted in 1905. The name "Montana" was added in 1981, and other changes were made in 1985.

Montana's state seal was officially adopted in 1865 but revised in 1893 after Montana became a state. It shows the words "The Great Seal of the State of Montana" in a circle on a brown field. Inside the circle are tools symbolizing Montana's mining and farming economy—a plow, shovel, and pick. A landscape of mountains, the sun, and the Great Falls of the Missouri River form the background behind the tools. At the bottom is the state motto, *Oro y Plata*, which is Spanish for "gold and silver."

"Montana" became the state song on February 20, 1945. The words were written by Charles Cohan and the music by Joseph Howard in 1910. They offered to donate sales of the song's sheet music to charity, and Montana's Children's Hospital in Helena was selected. The hospital is now named Shodair Children's Hospital. To view the lyrics, visit: **montanakids.com/facts_and_figures/ state_symbols/State_Song.htm.**

Glossary

badlands	An area where natural forces have worn away the soft rocks into sharp shapes and where plant life is scarce.
confluence	A place where things meet, used especially to describe where rivers and streams connect.
drought	A long period of very dry weather.
ecosystem	A community of organisms and their environment functioning as an ecological unit.
hydroelectric	Using the power of flowing water to produce electricity.
immigrants	People who come to live permanently in a foreign country.
missiles	Large weapons that are shot off, such as rockets.
mushers	People who lead teams of dogs to travel over snow.
National Historic Site	A building or place that is important in history and that is recognized and protected by the US government.
ore	Solid material found in nature from which a metal or valuable mineral can be removed.
palladium	A rare, shiny, lightweight, silvery-white metal used to make jewelry.
pharmacist	A person who is professionally qualified to measure and give out drugs used for medicine.
pronghorn	A deer-like animal with a stocky body, long, slim legs, and black horns that are shed and regrown annually.
ratified	Officially approved, as a law or a constitution, usually by a vote.
reservoir	A place (such as a lake, usually man-made) that is used to store a large supply of water for people to use for their needs.
tornadoes	Violent and destructive storms in which powerful winds move around a central point.
transmission lines	Cables designed to carry electricity over long distances.

More About Montana

BOOKS

Glynn, Gary. *Historic Photos of Montana*. Nashville, TN: Turner, 2009.

Josephson, Judith Pinkerton. *Who Was Sitting Bull? and Other Questions about the Battle of Little Bighorn*. Six Questions of American History. Minneapolis, MN: Lerner, 2011.

Naden, Corinne J. *Jeannette Rankin*. Leading Women. New York: Cavendish Square Publishing, 2012.

Smith, Roland. *The Captain's Dog: My Journey with the Lewis and Clark Tribe*. New York: Houghton Mifflin Harcourt, 2008.

WEBSITES

Montana Kids

montanakids.com

Montana's Official State Travel Site

www.visitmt.com

Montana's Official State Website

mt.gov

ABOUT THE AUTHORS

Ruth Bjorklund lives on Bainbridge Island, a ferry ride from Seattle, Washington, with her husband, children, and pets. She has contributed to many volumes in this series.

Gerry Boehme graduated from the Newhouse School at Syracuse University and lives on Long Island with his wife and two children. He is a published author and editor, a businessperson, and a guest speaker at national and international conferences.

Ellen H. Todras is a freelance writer and editor who loves history and enjoys brining it to life for children. She lives with her husband in Eugene, Oregon.

Index

Page numbers in **boldface** are illustrations. Entries in **boldface** are glossary terms.

Index